Teen Confidence Revolution

Teen Confidence Revolution

A Guide to Crush Negativity, Boost Self-Esteem,
Reduce Stress, and Slay Your Goals!

THE WORKBOOK

By Teen Powerhouse Society

Copyrighted Material

© Copyright 2024 - All rights reserved.

The content contained within this book may not be reproduced, duplicated or transmitted without direct written permission from the author or the publisher.

Under no circumstances will any blame or legal responsibility be held against the publisher, or author, for any damages, reparation, or monetary loss due to the information contained within this book, either directly or indirectly.

Legal Notice:

This book is copyright-protected. It is only for personal use. You cannot amend, distribute, sell, use, quote, or paraphrase any part, or the content within this book, without the consent of the author or publisher.

Disclaimer Notice:

Please note the information contained within this document is for educational and entertainment purposes only. All effort has been executed to present accurate, up-to-date, reliable, and complete information. No warranties of any kind are declared or implied. Readers acknowledge that the author is not engaged in the rendering of legal, financial, medical, or professional advice. The content within this book has been derived from various sources. Please consult a licensed professional before attempting any techniques outlined in this book.

By reading this document, the reader agrees that under no circumstances is the author responsible for any losses, direct or indirect, that are incurred as a result of the use of the information contained within this document, including, but not limited to, errors, omissions, or inaccuracies.

Dedication

To our beloved students. You have been the heartbeat of our days. From the tentative steps of ninth grade to the confident strides of twelfth, we have walked hand in hand. Weaving together threads of learning, laughter, and love. Your journey of self-discovery has been the greatest privilege to witness.

In your presence, we've found days of inspiration, frustration, gratitude, humor, and above all love. You have been our teachers, as much as we have been yours, and for that,
we are endlessly grateful.

As you step into the vast expanse of the world beyond the walls of the classroom, our deepest wish is for you to carry the essence of your unique magic with you. May you be happy, not just in fleeting moments, but in the quiet spaces between. May you be successful, not just in the eyes of the world, but in the whispers of your own heart. And, most importantly, may you be whole human beings, for your completeness is what will heal the world.

Find The Link To Your Free Bonus Goodies Inside!

Exclusive Printable Sticker Page
Printable Affirmation Cards

Contents

Introduction: Igniting The Teen Confidence Revolution

PART ONE: BOOST SELF-ESTEEM

Navigating The Journey Of Self-Discovery	1
Identifying Your Strengths	4
What's Your Worldview	6
List Your Goals...............Anything Goes	7
Identifying Your Values	8
The Values Treasure Hunt	9
Values Reflection	10
Draw Your Values Map	12
Values Map	13
Attuning To Your Feelings	14
The Great Digital Escape	15
The Great Digital Escape Reflection Questions	16
Social Media Check	17
Unique You	18
I Am A Gift To The World!	19

Contents

PART TWO: REDUCE STRESS

Dealing With The Inner Critic	20
Negative To Positive Thought Reframe	22
Self-Image	26
Your Confidence Movie Real	27
Spellbound Confidence Crafting Wizardry With Affirmations	29
Gratitude	34
Letters Through Time Past, Present, Future Me	35
Random Acts Of Kindness	37
25 Ways To Spread Kindness	38
Stress	40
Seven Steps To Demystify Stress	41
Stress Busters	44
Deep Breathing	44
Mindful Meditation	45
Creative Outlets	47
The Stress-Busting Trifecta Sleep, Eat, Move!	48
Health Habits Tracker	49

Contents

PART THREE: ACHIEVE GOALS

Goal Setting 50

SMARTER Goal Technique 51

PACT Goal Technique 51

WOOP Goal Technique 53

HARD Goal Technique 54

Goal Worksheets 56

Resilience Muscles 60

Strength Stones 62

Growth Mindset 64

Tree Of Growth 65

Strategies For Success 67

  The Power Of Yet 68

  I Believe In The Power Of Yet 69

  Yet-O-Meter 70

Contents

PART FOUR: CREATING A SUPPORTIVE TRIBE

The Power Of Connection 71

Mapping Your Support System 72

Passions And Dreams 75

The Role Of Fear And Insecurity 77

Create Your Confidence Revolution Community 79

Confidence Revolution Manifesto 82

Igniting The Teen Confidence Revolution

Welcome to a journey that transcends the pages of this book—a journey crafted especially for you, the courageous teenager navigating the maze of adolescence. In these pivotal years, as you stand on the threshold of self-discovery, we invite you to embark on a transformative adventure—your *Teen Confidence Revolution*.

In the realms of teenage life, where each day unveils a new challenge and a fresh opportunity, confidence becomes the compass guiding you through the ups and downs. Teen Powerhouse Society was born as a result of a 20-year veteran teacher husband and wife team, dedicated to empowering teenagers. We have been committed to helping teens navigate a less-than-ideal system all while staying true to who they are as the people they are and are becoming. This workbook is an invitation to *revolutionize* how you perceive yourself and your capabilities; it is a dynamic workbook with activities that are carefully designed to spark a fire inside of you to go beyond the ordinary and delve into the extraordinary potential that resides within you.

Our journey is divided into four parts—Boosting Self-Esteem, Reducing Stress, Achieving Goals, and Creating A Supportive Tribe—each a cornerstone in the construction of your confidence. In this book, you will learn how to crush the negativity that pervades each cornerstone once and for all! From creating your Confidence Manifesto to exploring the depths of your passions, from crafting affirmations that will empower you, to unlocking the secrets of goal-setting, each activity is a stepping stone in this grand adventure.

As you turn the pages, envision this not as a traditional book, but as a conversation between friends that celebrates your uniqueness, embraces your vulnerabilities, and propels you toward a future where confidence is not just a trait but a way of life. Prepare to be engaged, challenged, and inspired. Your *Teen Confidence Revolution* begins here and now, within these pages, but we hope its impact will resonate far beyond.

Open your heart to the possibilities, dare to dream, and let the revolution unfold—one transformative activity at a time. Are you ready to embark on this exhilarating journey? The path to confidence awaits, and the revolution begins with you.

Navigating The Journey Of Self-Discovery

During this transformative journey, we encourage you to explore the depths of your thoughts. Life is a grand adventure filled with twists, turns, and unexpected discoveries. Asking yourself questions and spending time answering them with love and intention, is like holding a lantern that will illuminate the path to self-discovery and empowerment. So grab your journal, find a quiet space, and let's explore together.

Introduce Yourself

What is your current age and a brief description of who you are? Think about the things you enjoy, your passions, and what makes you unique.

_____
_____
_____
_____
_____
_____
_____
_____
_____
_____
_____
_____
_____

Now, let's dig into ten questions designed to spark self-reflection. Take your time with each question, and don't be afraid to be honest and open with yourself.

What are your proudest achievements so far, big or small?

_____

_____

_____

Describe a moment when you felt truly confident. What where you doing, and how did it make you feel?

_____

_____

_____

What activities or hobbies bring you joy and make you lose track of time?

_____

_____

_____

Think about someone you admire. What qualities do they possess that you wish to cultivate in yourself?

_____

_____

_____

What challenges or fears are currently holding you back from reaching your full potential?

_____

_____

_____

Consider the last time you faced adversity. How did you overcome it, and what did you learn about yourself in the process?
_____
_____
_____

If you had unlimited confidence, what goals or dreams would you pursue?
_____
_____
_____

What negative thoughts or beliefs about yourself would you like to overcome?
_____
_____
_____

What do you believe your strengths to be? What have your parents, peers, or teachers told you that you are good at?
_____
_____
_____

What challenges or fears are currently holding you back from reaching your full potential?
_____
_____
_____

Identifying Your Strengths

Acknowledge your strengths for valuable insight into understanding your passions and what you are good at. **Instructions:** Rate yourself in the following areas by placing a number; 1 being the lowest and 5 being the highest in the corresponding box.

Personal Qualities	Self-Rating (1-5)
Communicative	
Empathetic	
Resourceful	
Adaptable	
Creative	
Resilient	
Assertive	
Motivated	
Independent	
Curious	
Open-minded	
Responsible	
Organized	
Optimistic	
Decisive	
Proactive	

Personal Qualities	Self-Rating (1-5)
Collaborative	
Inquisitive	
Patient	
Tenacious	
Perceptive	
Tolerant	
Altruistic	
Courageous	
Self-disciplined	
Reflective	
Honest	
Positive	
Punctual	
Analytical	
Goal-oriented	
Flexible	
Sociable	
Humble	

After you have completed, for those strengths that you rated yourself a 5, choose your top 5 strengths that you feel **best** describe you. List each strength below, then write down two examples of how you have demonstrated that strength.

Tip: In the next few days, ask people who know you well for their feedback if you have trouble deciding or just to confirm what you thought.

1. Strength

2. Strength

3. Strength

4. Strength

5. Strength

What's Your Worldview

Determine your worldview. Your worldview is often influenced by culture, family, and community. Everyone sees things differently and the lens through which you see the world provides insights into your identity. How do you see the world, with all its beauty, diversity, events, threats, and problems?

_____
_____
_____
_____
_____
_____
_____
_____
_____
_____
_____
_____
_____
_____

List Your Goals... Anything Goes

Determine your goals. For this page in your journey **simply list** all the things you have dreamed of accomplishing one day in your future. Do not allow yourself to be limited by current circumstances, not having enough money, or thinking you don't have what it takes.

Your goals forecast the kind of life you'd like to live in the future and they indicate where your passions lie.

Later, you will choose goals that you want to start getting serious about and use a goal-setting tool to help you achieve them.

- [ ] _____
- [ ] _____
- [ ] _____
- [ ] _____
- [ ] _____
- [ ] _____
- [ ] _____
- [ ] _____
- [ ] _____
- [ ] _____
- [ ] _____
- [ ] _____
- [ ] _____
- [ ] _____

Identifying Your Values

Next up, identify your core values. I know "core values" might sound like something from a corporate seminar, but trust me, discovering your values is like finding the *North Star* of your **authenticity.** While values may change over time, they are all part of what makes you the person you are at every stage of your development.

The Values Treasure Hunt

Imagine your values as *hidden treasures* within a vast landscape. Our job is to embark on a treasure hunt to uncover the gems that define who you are.

1. Circle Potential Values

Begin by using the list of potential values – qualities that could be your treasures. Things like kindness, creativity, courage, and curiosity; **circle** the ones that catch your eye or resonate with you. These are your clues.

2. Explore Your Landmarks:

Now, **wander** through your values landscape. For each circled value, jot down a memory, an experience, or a person that comes to mind. How has this value shown up in your life? How did it make you feel?

3. Choose Your Top Treasures:

After exploring, **narrow down your list to the top values** that feel most significant to you. These are your core treasures, the values that guide your decisions, shape your character, and make you who you are.

4. Draw Your Values Map :

Finally, have some fun **drawing a treasure map** in your journal, or use the one provided as a reference. Make it as **imaginative and colorful** as you like. Your map represents the landscape of your values, and each landmark represents what is most important to you.

The Values Treasure Hunt

Circle the values that *most* resonate with you.

Authenticity
Compassion
Resilience
Integrity
Kindness
Generosity
Gratitude
Curiosity
Empathy
Creativity
Courage
Friendship
Optimism
Adventurousness
Responsibility
Determination
Ambition
Honesty
Independence
Mindfulness
Patience
Humility
Tolerance
Acceptance
Peace

Justice
Teamwork
Leadership
Self-Reflection
Perseverance
Balance
Flexibility
Loyalty
Open-mindedness
Sense of Humor
Positivity
Self-Respect
Self-Confidence
Sincerity
Innovation
Health
Environmental Consciousness
Caring for Others
Fairness
Security
Freedom
Family
Education
Achievement
Fun/Playfulness
Honor

Values Reflection

Choose 6 values. Write the value at the top of the box. Next write the memory, experience, or person that comes to mind and how did it make you feel? How does this value show up in your life? If you need more space to write or journal use the next page.

Draw Your Values Map

No need to overthink this; just get started. **It's not about what it looks like in the end** but about the **process, ideas, and insights you uncover.**

Values Map

Attuning To Your Feelings

When you pay attention to your feelings you are more likely to develop **healthy coping mechanisms**, instead of suppressing emotions or resorting to negative behaviors. Tracking your feelings promotes self-reflection and over time, you can assess patterns, identify triggers, and work towards personal growth. It encourages a proactive approach to emotional well-being.

Use the mood tracker provided and assign colors to different emotions to create a color-coded system. Put a number in each circle to represent the day of the month. Then color in the circle with the color that represents your predominant emotion for that day. See what emerges over the next month.

Color System

The Great Digital Escape

So our dear tech-savvy rebels! Welcome to the ultimate quest for freedom in a world obsessed with pixels and pings. We know you're the kings and queens of swipes and double-taps, but ever felt like your digital kingdom is taking over your real-life castle? Fear not, brave souls, because it's time for *The Great Digital Escape!*

We invite you for 1 week to ditch the screens, emojis, and endless scrolling for a chance to rediscover what it means to be human without the constant hum of notifications. Picture this: a world where your day isn't dictated by the glow of a screen but by the warmth of real connections and the thrill of tangible experiences.

Prepare for a tech-free week, where the only status you'll be checking is the one you set for yourself. It's a *digital detox*, and it's about to revolutionize the way you see the world—beyond filters and hashtags. Buckle up, because this is your chance to break free from the shackles of the virtual universe and embark on a quest for self-discovery, real connections, and maybe even a few surprises along the way.

So, dear revolutionary, are you ready to smash the digital matrix and discover what lies beyond the blue light? *The Great Digital Escape* awaits, and it's time for you to reclaim your throne in the kingdom of reality! Seriously, you need to try this. Get a friend or two to join you and compare your experiences.

After your week offline use the questions on the next page to reflect on your experience. Express your thoughts openly and honestly, answers are personal and there's no right or wrong answer. These questions are designed to you gain insights into your digital habits, relationships, and overall well-being during *The Great Digital Escape*.

The Great Digital Escape: Reflection Questions

1. What surprised you the most about your week without digital devices?

2. How did the absence of social media impact your daily routine and overall mood?

3. What offline activities brought you the most joy or satisfaction?

4. Did you notice any changes in your relationships with friends and family during the digital detox?

5. In what ways did the digital detox influence your perspective on technology and its role in your life?

Social Media Check

Remember that the internet and social media are *not* a bad thing but too much of it can leave you missing out on **your** real life. Escaping the pressures of social media is crucial for teens to maintain confidence and positive self-esteem. Here are strategies you can employ after your detox to continue a healthy balance:

Establish Boundaries:
Set specific time limits for social media usage. Create a schedule that allows designated periods for social media and ensures time for other activities, such as homework, hobbies, and face-to-face interactions.

Digital Detox:
Consider periodic digital detoxes. Designate days or weekends where you intentionally disconnect from social media. This break provides an opportunity to focus on offline activities and relationships.

Selective Engagement:
Be selective in your social media engagement. Know when it's time to unfollow accounts that contribute to negative feelings or unrealistic standards. Cultivate a positive online environment.

Real-Life Connections:
Prioritize real-life connections. Face-to-face interactions with friends and family are valuable to your growth. These connections offer genuine support and a sense of belonging.

Hobbies and Passions:
Identify and pursue offline hobbies and passions. Engage in activities that you love to provide a sense of fulfillment and achievement outside the digital realm.

Self-Esteem Building:
Focus on building self-esteem independent of online validation. By doing the work in this book and developing yourself you are finding value in your skills, talents, and personal growth rather than relying on social media likes or comments for validation.

Unique You

Listen, teens, we get it, navigating the labyrinth of adolescence can feel like walking in circles through waves of self-doubt and comparison. But what if we told you that your quirks, your vibes, and that oh-so-unique essence of you are the secret sauce to building confidence?

Your journey isn't about fitting into molds—it's about breaking them, one dazzling quirk at a time. Take some time to discover the magic within and sprinkle your unique stardust.

Embracing your uniqueness is the ultimate superhero move. It's time to drop the comparison game and instead, unleash the power of self-love and acceptance. Uncover why being your fabulously quirky self is the key to unlocking confidence.

Please remember that through this journey practicing self-compassion is **essential.** Accept that being different is a strength, not a weakness. Treat yourself with the kindness and understanding you deserve. Self-love is the key to embracing what makes you unique. On the next page complete the activity to discover why you are a gift to the world.

I Am A Gift To The World!

Time to get creative revolutionaries! The *I Am a Gift to the World Collage* is an empowering activity, to explore and celebrate your uniqueness. The goal is to create a visual collage that reflects your individuality and showcases the gifts you bring to the world. Commit to creating collages of your teen years so you can see just how much you have to celebrate and share with the world.

Materials Needed:
1. Magazines, newspapers, or printouts with images and words
2. Scissors
3. Glue or tape
4. Poster board or a large sheet of paper
5. Markers, colored pencils, or pens
6. Stickers, glitter, or any additional decorative materials (optional)

Instructions:
1. **Self-Reflection:** Begin the activity with a moment of self-reflection. Ponder and jot down qualities, interests, strengths, and passions that make you unique.
2. **Collage Elements Hunt:** Use magazines, newspapers, or printouts containing images and words. Search for visuals and text that resonate with your self-reflection. Find elements that represent your interests, aspirations, and the essence of who you are.
3. **Cut and Arrange:** Using scissors, cut out the chosen images and words. Arrange these elements on the poster board or large sheet of paper in a way that feels visually pleasing and meaningful to you. **Let go of perfectionism!**
4. **Reflective Writing:** Once you are done write a short reflection about your collage on the back of it. What do the chosen elements symbolize? How do these pieces come together to represent their uniqueness?
5. **Optional:** Share and Discuss your collage with family or friends. This way you can build and maintain positive and supportive discussions about the diverse qualities you bring to the world.

Affirm your self-worth and uniqueness. Remember **do the work!** This activity will be a visual reminder of the incredible gifts that you bring to the world.

Dealing With The Inner-Critic

So, you've stepped into the realm of criticism, where judgmental arrows fly like confetti at a surprise party. Here's the real kicker: it's not just external critique; your *Inner Critic* joins the party too. But guess what? Before facing the outside world, you've got to do some inner housekeeping. Wrangle that *Inner Critic* and make it your ally. Let's turn criticism into your trusty sidekick on this epic journey. Can you believe it? Criticism as a friend, there to lend a helping hand? Turn it into your friendly mentor, not a foe. Picture this: a collaborative conversation where you're not here to clash but to level up together.

Read the following conversation and on the blank page that follows, allow yourself to write the conversation you have with your inner critic.

Inner Critic vs. Teen: An Unexpected Truce

Setting: Teen's Bedroom, Late Evening

Teen (T): (Sitting on the bed, contemplating a new opportunity) I don't know if I should take this chance. It feels scary.

Inner Critic (IC): (Appearing with a worried expression) Scary? More like downright terrifying. You really want to put yourself out there? What if you fail?

T: (Nervously) I know, but it could also be an amazing opportunity. I don't want to let fear hold me back.

IC: Fear is there for a reason, you know. It's trying to keep you safe. Taking risks is dangerous.

T: (Understanding) I get that you're just looking out for me, trying to keep me safe. I appreciate that. But I also want to grow and experience new things.

IC: (Skeptical) Grow? Experience? You can do that without taking big risks. What if things go wrong?

T: (Smiling) I hear you, and I know you're trying to protect me. But I want to try. Even if it's scary, I want to see what happens.

IC: (Softening) I just don't want you to get hurt. You mean a lot to me.

T: (Gratefully) Thank you for caring. I promise I'll be cautious, but I need to step out of my comfort zone sometimes.

IC: (Reluctantly) Fine, but be careful. And if things get too intense, don't hesitate to retreat.

T: (Nodding) I will. Thanks for looking out for me, even if it means being scared for a little while.

IC: (Fading away) Just remember, I'll be here if you need me.

Negative to Postive Thought Reframe

Now your *Inner Critic* is a tricky companion; sometimes they can be a real downer. There are days when it won't just be a gentle nudge; it might feel more like a hurricane of negativity. But always remember that you've got the power to turn the storm into a gentle breeze.

When the *Inner Critic* gets a bit too loud and overbearing, it's time to reframe those negative thoughts into positive ones. Picture it like adjusting the lens through which you view yourself and the world. Here's your escape plan:

Step 1: Identify the Negative Thought

First, catch that sneaky negative thought. Pin it down like a butterfly in a net. What exactly is it saying? Write it down if you have to—sometimes putting it on paper makes it easier to tackle.

Step 2: Question the Critic

Now, it's interrogation time! Ask yourself: "Is this thought based on facts or feelings?" Often, our inner critic exaggerates and distorts reality. Challenge it by seeking evidence for or against the negative thought.

Step 3: Challenge and Reframe

Turn the tables on that inner critic. Ask yourself, "What's a more positive way to look at this?" Let's say your inner critic says, "I always mess things up." Challenge it with, "I've faced challenges before, and I've learned and grown from them. This is just another opportunity to learn."

Step 4: What Would a Friend Say?

Imagine your best friend or someone you care about is going through the same situation. What would you say to them? Now, say that to yourself. Treat yourself with the same kindness and encouragement you'd offer a friend.

Step 5: Focus on Solutions

Shift from dwelling on the problem to finding solutions. Instead of getting stuck in, "I can't do this," explore, "What small step can I take to make progress?" You're not aiming for perfection—just progress.

Remember, you're the boss of your thoughts. Reframing takes practice, but each time you do it, you're rewriting the script of how you see yourself. So, when that *Inner Critic* gets a bit too rowdy, show it who's boss and lead the way to a more positive and empowering reality. You've got this!

Let's go Deeper

Our thoughts are always with us so paying attention to reframing them is important to build resilience. To make this superpower a habit, consider diving a bit deeper. Take a moment to answer these critical questions whenever you catch those pesky negative thoughts trying to sneak in. **Use the pages that follow to journal some of this out.**

Test how realistic your thoughts are:
- Is there credible evidence to support this idea?
- If you were to objectively evaluate your thoughts, could you discredit them?
- Why should I trust my negative predictions of the future?

See the bigger picture:
- What's the worst thing that could happen?
- What's the best thing that could happen?
- What's most likely to happen, based on the information I have?
- Is there anything good about this situation?
- Will this matter in five years?

Self-Image

Let's chat about a power player in the world of teen confidence—self-image. Yep, that mental Polaroid we carry around of ourselves. Now, it's not always as Instagrammable as we'd like, but fear not! We've got the scoop on how to turn that mental selfie into a masterpiece.

Picture your self-image as the director of your personal blockbuster movie, starring—you guessed it—YOU! It's got a script filled with highs, lows, and those in-between moments. How you see yourself affects your confidence, it also affects your relationships with others... who's going to want a backstage VIP pass to the **Your Name Here Confidence Show** if you are struggling with self-image?

Self-image isn't just about looks; it's the vibe you give off to the world. If your mental movie constantly plays a reel of doubts and insecurities, it's time for a script rewrite. Your confidence deserves a leading role, not a supporting act.

Your Confidence Movie Reel

Bring your confidence journey to life through a short and easy-to-create movie reel. This activity lets you visualize your growth and celebrate moments of strength in a dynamic and engaging format.

Materials Needed:

Smartphone or camera
Basic video editing software or apps (e.g., iMovie, Adobe Premiere Clip)
Positive Affirmation Playlist (Create a list of empowering songs)
Mirror

Instructions:

1. Script Your Scenes:

Outline key scenes that represent your confidence journey. These could include moments of personal growth, achievements, or instances where you demonstrated resilience. Keep it simple and use 3 to 5 scenes.

2. Capture the Moments:

Using your smartphone or camera, record short clips for each scene. **Don't worry about perfection; authenticity is key.**

3. Empowering Playlist:

Every movie needs music right? Create a playlist of empowering songs. Choose tracks that resonate with your journey and will enhance the emotional impact of your movie reel.

4. Mirror Reflection:

Intersperse your recording sessions with moments of reflection in front of the mirror. Share your thoughts, feelings, and aspirations for each scene.

5. Edit with Flair:

Use basic video editing software or apps to compile your clips. Add transitions, music, and simple effects to enhance the storytelling aspect of your movie reel.

6. Narrate Your Story:

If you feel comfortable, record a brief narration for your movie reel. Share insights, lessons learned, and how each scene contributes to your evolving confidence story.

7. Premiere Night:

Plan a "premiere night" to watch your confidence movie reel. Invite friends or family to join you, creating a supportive and celebratory atmosphere. Consider sharing your confidence movie reel on social media or with a trusted community. Your story might inspire others on their confidence journeys.

As you continue to grow and achieve, update your movie reel. Add new scenes to showcase the ongoing evolution of your confidence. This activity transforms your confidence journey into a dynamic and shareable movie reel, allowing you to visually capture and celebrate moments of growth, strength, and resilience.

Spellbound Confidence: Crafting Wizardry With Affirmations

Ready to sprinkle a little magic onto your self-esteem journey? Get ready to craft your very own affirmations—your secret weapon against doubt and the ultimate confidence boost. **Let's unlock the door to positive self-talk.**

Words are often likened to spells because, like magic incantations, they have the power to shape reality, influence emotions, and impact our perceptions. The idea behind this analogy is rooted in the profound effect words can have on our thoughts and feelings. Let's use this **magical metaphor** to create your affirmations.

Step 1: Summon Your Inner Wordsmith

Imagine you're a wizard casting a spell, but instead of a wand, you're armed with words. Affirmations are your incantations, so channel your inner wordsmith and let the magic flow. Start by summoning positive phrases that resonate with your goals and aspirations.

"*I am a beacon of awesomeness*," or "**Every challenge is an opportunity in disguise.**" Go on, weave words that make you feel invincible.

Step 2: Brew a Potion of Positivity

In the cauldron of your mind, mix a potion of positivity. Choose words that spark joy and strength. "**I radiate confidence like a supernova**," or "**I am the architect of my success.**" Stir in some self-love and watch the potion bubble with empowerment.

Step 3: Create a Daily Spellbook

Every wizard needs a spellbook, right? Think of your affirmation journal as your magical grimoire. Write down affirmations frequently, and revisit them daily.

Step 4: Enchant Your Environment

Spread the magic! Post your affirmations where you'll see them—on your mirror, the fridge, or even as your phone wallpaper. Let them seep into your surroundings, turning your space into a portal of confidence.

Step 5: Level Up with Action

Affirmations are your allies, but even wizards need to wield their magic wisely. Combine your words with actions. If your affirmation is, **"I am a powerhouse of determination,"** show it by tackling challenges head-on. Your actions will make the magic even more potent.

Remember, you're not just creating affirmations; you're crafting spells that transform self-doubt into self-belief. So, grab your quill, tap into your wizardry, and let the confidence enchantments begin!

It's important to note that while the comparison between words and spells is metaphorical, the essence lies in recognizing the transformative power of language. Words can indeed be magical in the way they shape our perceptions, attitudes, and ultimately, our reality.

Certificate of Recognition

THE FOLLOWING AWARD IS GIVEN TO

This certificate is given to the revolutionary who has come this far in the process of boosting self-esteem, reducing stress, and achieving goals. You are at the halfway point of the book and if you have completed all the exercises honor yourself by printing this and writing your name to prove that you have what it takes to follow through on your Teen Confidence Revolution!

_____   _____
          Witness   Witness

JOIN THE CONFIDENCE REVOLUTION!
UNLEASH YOUR GENEROSITY POWER

Hey there, amazing revolutionary reader! How do you like the workbook so far?

Do you believe in the power of generosity? Well, guess what? You have a chance to make a real difference in someone's life, and it'll only take a minute of your time.

Imagine helping a fellow teenager overcome self-doubt, low self-esteem, and negativity. Picture them breaking free to pursue their dreams, express themselves, and interact with others. That's the potential impact of your review of ***Teen Confidence Revolution Workbook: A Guide To Crush Negativity, Boost Self-Esteem, Reduce Stress, And Slay Your Goals!*** by Teen Powerhouse Society.

Our mission is to make this empowering book accessible to everyone, and we need your help. Your review can be the guiding light for someone who, just like you, is eager to make a positive change but might not know where to start.

Will you join us in this mission? We believe that your generous act of leaving a review can transform lives. Your words could be the encouragement someone needs to:

- Build self-confidence and embrace their uniqueness. Manage stress and navigate the challenges of modern life.
- Set and achieve meaningful goals.
- Share the gift of confidence with others in their community.

Here's your chance to be part of a revolution that promotes positivity, growth, and support among teenagers. Your review is a small action that can lead to big, meaningful changes for someone out there.

Ready to spread the word? It's easy! Simply scan the QR code below or visit [https://www.amazon.com/review/review-your-purchases/?asin=B0CSDRLBT2] to share your thoughts about the book.

By leaving a review, you're not just sharing your opinion; **you're contributing to a movement that empowers teens** to reach their full potential.

If you're on Audible Hit the three dots at the top right of your device click rate and review, then leave a few sentences about the book with a star rating.

If you are on Kindle or an eReader scroll to the bottom of the book then swipe up and it will prompt you to leave a review.

If for some reason these instructions have changed, simply go to Amazon or wherever you purchase the book and leave a review right on the books page. For Amazon, click here.

Thank you from the Teen Powerhouse Society!

Your generosity is valued beyond measure. We can't wait to continue this journey with you, unlocking more strategies to boost self-esteem, reduce stress, and help you achieve your goals.

Remember, your review isn't just about a book; it's about creating a ripple effect of confidence that can change lives. So, thank you for being a part of something incredible!

Warm regards,
Teen Powerhouse Society

PS - Share the positivity! If you know someone who could benefit from this book, send it their way and let's spread the *Teen Confidence Revolution* together.

Now go download your free goodies and keep reading!

Free Bonus Goodies!

Please type this link into your browser, enter your email, and download your freebies: https://mailchi.mp/b9d658d8aa59/teenpowerhousesociety

Exclusive Printable Sticker Page
Printable Affirmation Cards

Gratitude

Practicing gratitude means turning your mental lens to focus on the awesome stuff, big or small, happening around you. When you are feeling overwhelmed by the challenges life throws your way gratitude swoops in like a superhero, helping you navigate stress by shifting your focus to what's going right.

Sometimes it's a good idea to keep a gratitude journal to write three things you are grateful for daily. If you can't get around to that you can use copies of the page below to boost your satisfaction and happiness in life.

GRATITUDE JOURNAL

Date:

Today, I'm Grateful For:

_____
_____
_____
_____

One thing I can do to step out of my comfort zone this week?

Something I'm Proud Of:

Things I am Looking Forward:

Today's Affirmation:

Letters Through Time: Past, Present, and Future Me

Continue your journey of self-discovery and self-acceptance by writing heartfelt letters to your past, present, and future selves. This activity is a powerful tool to reflect on your growth, acknowledge your present strengths, and set positive intentions for the future.

Materials Needed:

Paper
Pens or markers
Quiet and comfortable space

Instructions:

1. Letter to Your Past Self:

Reflect on your past, both the proud moments and those that taught you valuable lessons. Begin your letter by addressing your past self. Share specific events or experiences you are proud of, acknowledging the achievements and strengths that shaped you. Move on to moments that might have been challenging or taught you important lessons. Be compassionate and understanding as you reflect on these times.

2. Letter to Your Present Self:

Shift your focus to the present moment. Consider the person you are today, recognizing the growth and positive qualities you possess.
In your letter to your present self, celebrate your achievements, no matter how small. Acknowledge your strengths, resilience, and the unique qualities that make you who you are. Express gratitude for the journey you've undertaken and take a moment to revel in the person you've become.

3. Letter to Your Future Self:

Envision the person you want to become by the end of the school year. What goals do you want to achieve? What qualities do you want to develop further? In your letter to your future self, set positive intentions. Outline the achievements you aspire to reach, the personal growth you want to experience, and the steps you'll take to get there. Seal this letter with hope and excitement for the journey ahead.

4. Reflection and Closure:

After completing the letters, take a moment to reflect on the emotions that surfaced during the process. Consider sharing excerpts from your letters with a trusted friend or family member, teacher, coach, counselor, or mentor to allow yourself to be seen and celebrated.

Letters Through Time is a therapeutic and empowering way to foster self-acceptance, celebrate your journey, and set positive intentions for the future.

Random Acts of Kindness

Revolutionary teen, we have a mission for you that not only makes the world brighter but also supercharges your confidence... Brace yourselves for the extraordinary power of kindness – your secret weapon to increasing your well-being and transforming not only the world around you but also your own mental and emotional landscape.

The Kindness/Confidence Connection:

Did you know that being kind isn't just about making others feel good? It's also a potent source of personal empowerment! Here's the secret sauce: when you spread kindness, it sends ripples of positivity into the universe, and those ripples bounce right back to boost your self-esteem.

Have you ever noticed that warm, fuzzy feeling after helping someone? That's your mood doing a happy dance! Acts of kindness release endorphins, the feel-good hormones, making you instantly happier. Furthermore, small acts of generosity trigger the release of oxytocin, the "love hormone," reducing stress and promoting a sense of calm.

There is just no possible way you could be sad when you are giving of yourself to others! When you connect with others through acts of kindness, you create a network of positive relationships. Feeling connected is a crucial component of your overall well-being.

Life can throw curveballs, but kindness equips you with the resilience to bounce back. The positive emotions generated by acts of kindness act as a shield against the challenges of daily life.

If you have ever thrown a pebble into a pond and watched the ripples spread that's kind of the same thing that acts of kindness create. The joy you bring to others amplifies, creating a positive atmosphere around you.

While spreading kindness, let it be your little secret. Why? Because genuine acts of kindness are about lifting others, not about seeking recognition. Your confidence boost will come from the joy you bring to others, not from a spotlight on your actions.

Ready to be a Kindness Crusader and watch your confidence soar?

25 Ways to Spread Kindness (Keep it on the Down Low!)

Leave an Encouraging Note: Slip a positive note into a friend's locker or backpack.

Compliment Avalanche: Shower compliments on those around you. Everyone loves a genuine compliment!

Random Act of Clean-Up: Tidy up a communal space without being asked. A little cleanliness can go a long way.

Tech-Free Time: Offer your undivided attention during conversations. Put away the phone and truly listen.

Surprise Snack Attack: Share a tasty treat with a friend or leave one on a peer's desk.

Volunteer Virtuoso: Offer your time to a local charity or community event. Your generosity will come back in waves.

Eco-Friendly Warrior: Clean up litter in your neighborhood or local park.

Forgiveness Ambassador: Let go of a grudge or forgive someone who may not even know they hurt you.

Virtual High-Five: Send an uplifting message to someone who might be going through a tough time.

Secret Santa Vibes: Leave a small gift or treat anonymously for a friend or family member.

Compassionate Ears: Be there for someone who needs to vent. Sometimes, a listening ear is the greatest gift.

Hold the Door: A simple act that goes a long way. Hold the door for someone and watch their face light up.

Gratitude Notes: Write thank-you notes for people who often go unnoticed, like janitors or cafeteria staff.

Positive Post-its: Stick uplifting notes in unexpected places for strangers to find.

Gardening Guru: Plant flowers in a public space to bring beauty to your community.

Drive-By Goodness: Leave a small treat on a neighbor's doorstep without revealing yourself.

Social Media Positivity: Share uplifting content on your social media platforms. Be a force for good online!

Book Fairy: Leave a favorite book in a public place with a note encouraging the finder to enjoy and pass it on.

Help a Classmate: Offer assistance to someone struggling with their homework or studies.

Laughter Ambassador: Share a funny meme or joke to brighten someone's day.

Meal Magic: Cook a meal for a friend or family member, or even a neighbor in need.

Encouraging Art: Create small, positive artworks and leave them in public spaces for others to discover.

Fitness Friend: Encourage someone to join you for a workout or a walk. Exercise is a mood booster!

Tip Generously: If you're in a position to do so, leave a generous tip for a service worker.

Kindness in the Mirror: Be kind to yourself. Practice self-love and self-care. You deserve it!

Stress

Stress – the sneaky villain that tries to mess with your groove. As you navigate the winding path of teenage life, think of stress as the challenging level in a video game – **conquerable with the right moves.** Teens, let's unravel the mystery behind stress and equip you with strategies to conquer everyday battles.

Stress often creeps in through various doorways, with academic pressure, social dynamics, future uncertainties, and the digital realm being common stressors. The avalanche of exams, the intricacies of friendships and relationships, the looming question of "What's next?", and the constant digital buzz can stir up the storm. However, fret not, as there are practical ways to navigate these stressors.

- Practice effective time-management; a key tool for tackling academic demands, and breaking down tasks into manageable portions.
- Cultivate positive relationships
- Set boundaries in the digital world to ease social and tech-related stress
- Embrace uncertainty about the future as a natural part of life's journey; it helps alleviate stress.

Incorporating small but impactful habits like deep breathing, maintaining a balanced routine, and seeking support from friends or family can go a long way in combating stress. So, teens, let's demystify stress, understand its triggers, and employ these solutions to pave the way for a smoother journey through adolescence.

7 Steps To Demystify Stress

Demystifying stress and understanding its triggers is like becoming a stress detective – you're Enola Holmes, but cooler. Here's your step-by-step guide to unravel the stress mystery:

Step 1: Identify the Stress Villains

Just like Enola identifies culprits, start by pinpointing stress triggers. What situations, tasks, or thoughts make your stress radar ping? It could be looming exams, social situations, or even future uncertainties. List them out like a seasoned detective listing suspects.

Step 2: Investigate Your Reactions

Now, channel your inner detective to investigate how you react to stress. Do you get jittery, feel overwhelmed, or maybe lose your cool? Understanding your reactions is key to cracking the stress code. It's like figuring out how your stress villains operate.

Step 3: Connect the Dots

Time to connect the dots! Analyze your list of stress triggers and reactions. Are there patterns? Maybe deadlines consistently stress you out, or social situations trigger anxious feelings. By connecting the dots, you're creating a stress map – a valuable tool for your teen toolkit.

Step 4: Journal Your Findings

Grab your detective notebook – a.k.a., your journal – and document your findings. Write down your stress triggers, reactions, and any patterns you've uncovered. This not only helps you remember your discoveries but also serves as a roadmap for stress-prevention strategies.

Step 5: Seek Witness Testimonies

Sometimes, you need witnesses to crack the case. Talk to friends, family, or a trusted teacher. They might offer valuable insights into your stress triggers that you hadn't considered. It's like gathering eyewitness accounts for the stress investigation.

Step 6: Experiment with Stress-Busting Strategies

Armed with your stress detective toolkit, experiment with stress-busting strategies. If looming exams are stress triggers, try breaking down study sessions. If social situations make your stress radar go haywire, practice positive self-talk. It's all about finding what disarms your stress villains.

Step 7: Evaluate and Adjust

Detective work is an ongoing process. Regularly evaluate your stress-busting strategies. Are they effective? Do you need to tweak your approach? Maybe a new stress trigger has emerged. Stay vigilant, adapt your strategies, and continue your journey as the ultimate stress detective.

So, there you have it – your guide to demystifying stress and understanding its triggers. Time to grab a pen, your metaphorical magnifying glass, put on your detective hat, and let the stress-solving adventures begin!

Stress Busters

Here are more specific strategies tailored just for you to manage stress like a pro.

Deep Breathing

The Technique: 4-7-8

Start by finding a quiet and comfortable space. Sit or lie down with your back straight and shoulders relaxed. This is your Zen Zone – your oasis of calm.

Empty the Lungs; close your eyes and take a deep breath in through your nose for a count of 4. Feel the air fill your lungs like a balloon inflating. Now, exhale completely through your mouth, making a whooshing sound, for a count of 8. Release any tension with each exhale.

Inhale again through your nose, this time for a count of 4. Allow the breath to be gentle and natural. Now, hold your breath for a count of 7. Feel the stillness, like a peaceful pause in the middle of a symphony.

Exhale with purpose through your mouth, making that whooshing sound once more, for a count of 8. Imagine releasing any lingering stress or negativity with each exhale. You're creating space for tranquility.

The Technique: Alternate Nostril Breathing:

Use your right thumb to close your right nostril and inhale deeply through your left nostril. Close your left nostril with your right ring finger, release your right nostril, and exhale. Inhale through your right nostril, close it, release your left nostril, and exhale. Repeat the cycle.

The Technique: Lions Breath

Inhale deeply through your nose. Exhale forcefully through your mouth, sticking out your tongue and roaring like a lion. Repeat for a few cycles, releasing tension and promoting a sense of playfulness.

Stress Busters

Mindful Meditation: "Inner Strength Activation"

Welcome to a world where **your voice** becomes the guiding light for stress reduction. You can find all kinds of meditations on YouTube but have you considered listening to your *own voice* for deeper internalization of stress relief?

Recording your own guided meditations adds a personal touch to your mindfulness journey. Use your smartphone or any recording device you have access to. **You don't need fancy equipment; simplicity is key.** Enhance your meditation with soft, ambient background sounds like nature sounds or gentle music if you like. And editing is optional but if you choose, you can access many free editing apps. Use the meditation below to help you on this venture. Just read this meditation slowly and clearly and give time for it to sink in, pause often as you record.

Introduction:

Welcome to **Inner Strength Activation,**" a guided mindful meditation designed to unlock your potential and boost your confidence. Find a comfortable and quiet space, and let's begin.

Guidance:

Close your eyes and take a few deep breaths, inhaling positivity and exhaling all tension. Picture yourself in a serene place—a calming beach, a peaceful forest, or any place you feel at ease. Imagine a warm, golden light surrounding you, radiating confidence and self-assurance. As you breathe in, feel this golden light entering your body, filling you with strength and courage.
With each exhale, release any self-doubt or negativity that may be holding you back.

Now, visualize a door in front of you. As you open it, step into a room filled with your greatest achievements and moments of triumph. Take your time and visualize each achievement one at a time. What have you accomplished? What makes you proud?

Stress Busters

Hear the applause, feel the joy, and bask in the glow of your accomplishments. You are capable, resilient, and deserving of success.
Affirm to yourself: "I am strong. I am confident. I believe in my abilities."

Conclusion:
Slowly bring your awareness back to the present moment. Carry this newfound confidence with you throughout your day. You possess incredible strength within—tap into it and watch yourself shine.

Now Journal About It! What came up for you as you listened to a recording of this mindful meditation?

_____
_____
_____
_____
_____
_____
_____
_____
_____
_____
_____
_____

By recording your guided meditation, you not only cultivate a valuable skill but also contribute to your well-being. Your voice becomes a beacon of tranquility in a sometimes chaotic world. Embrace the power of your own words and embark on this journey of self-expression and stress reduction.

Stress Busters

Take a look at the list of creative outlets to decompress and reduce stress:

Drawing/Painting
Writing
Photography
Music
Dancing
Cooking/Baking
Gardening
Graphic Design
DIY Crafts
Film-making
Sculpture
Pottery
Yoga
Coding
Podcasting
Acting
Poetry Slam
Graphic Novels
Fashion Design
Calligraphy
Astronomy
Puzzle Solving
Board Games
Hiking
Virtual Reality
Martial Arts
Stand-up Comedy
Mobile Apps/Games
Meditation
Origami

Creative Outlet

Choose your top 5 that you want to explore further!

Stress Busters

The Stress-Busting Trifecta: Sleep, Eat, Move!

Don't forget about your **foundational** stress-busting trio – sleep, eat, and move!

1. Snooze Like a Pro:

Ever heard the saying, "Early to bed, early to rise"? Turns out, it's not just for old folks. Quality sleep is your secret weapon against stress. Think of it as a superhero nap that recharges your mental batteries. So, dim the lights, power down your gadgets, and dive into dreamland. Your stress levels will thank you in the morning.

2. Eat the Rainbow:

No, we're not talking about Skittles; we mean a colorful plate! Load up on fruits, veggies, lean proteins, and whole grains. These superfoods are like the Avengers for your body, ready to battle stress villains. And hey, the occasional treat won't hurt – balance is the key. A well-fed revolutionary is a stress-resistant revolutionary!

3. Bust a Move – Literally:

Exercise is not just for gym rats; it's your ticket to stress relief. Whether it's dancing, jogging, or yoga, find what makes your body groove. Exercise releases magical chemicals called endorphins that fight off stress and boost your mood. Plus, it's a chance to break free from the daily grind – double win!

The stress-busting trifecta – sleep, eat, move – is your golden ticket to a chill life. Let's face each day with a smile, armed with the power of a good night's sleep, nutritious meals, and some exercise. Stress doesn't stand a chance against you!

A habit tracker makes turning these stress-busting tricks into daily, weekly, or monthly wins a breeze. It's your secret weapon to stay on top, beat stress, and unlock your confidence. Use the tracker that follows to this end.

Health Habits

WEEK OF _____

	MENU PLANNER	WORKOUT	WATER INTAKE
Monday	Breakfast Lunch Dinner Snacks	Exercise Calories Burned	💧💧💧💧💧 💧💧💧💧💧
Tuesday	Breakfast Lunch Dinner Snacks	Exercise Calories Burned	💧💧💧💧💧 💧💧💧💧💧
Wednesday	Breakfast Lunch Dinner Snacks	Exercise Calories Burned	💧💧💧💧💧 💧💧💧💧💧
Thursday	Breakfast Lunch Dinner Snacks	Exercise Calories Burned	💧💧💧💧💧 💧💧💧💧💧
Friday	Breakfast Lunch Dinner Snacks	Exercise Calories Burned	💧💧💧💧💧 💧💧💧💧💧
Saturday	Breakfast Lunch Dinner Snacks	Exercise Calories Burned	💧💧💧💧💧 💧💧💧💧💧
Sunday	Breakfast Lunch Dinner Snacks	Exercise Calories Burned	💧💧💧💧💧 💧💧💧💧💧

Goal-Setting

Ever find yourself adrift in the vast sea of the unknown, unsure of which course to chart? Never fear, for we're about to embark on a grand voyage that will transform the foggy waters of tomorrow into crystal-clear, confident horizons. Welcome aboard the ship of goal-setting!

Envision this: You're the captain of your odyssey, crafting the narrative of your life's epic saga. Goal-setting becomes your navigational chart, your compass guiding you through uncharted territories. It's not about rigid routes; it's about creating a roadmap, a north star to steer you through the boundless possibilities.

Setting goals isn't merely about grandiose dreams (*though those are like treasure chests of awesomeness*); it's about the small victories that ripple through your journey. It's the secret formula to boost confidence and declare to the world, "Behold, this is the path I tread!" just like when Disney's Moana said... "*I am Moana of Motunui. You will board my boat, sail across the ocean, and restore the heart of Te Fiti.*" Yes, she was declaring to the world her purpose and her confidence! It's time for you to do the same.

You won't navigate these waters alone; you'll be armed with four mighty tools – **SMARTER *goal technique*, PACT *goal technique*, WOOP *goal technique*, and HARD *goal technique*.** These aren't just fancy acronyms; they're your companions, helping you chart a course that's both thrilling and purposeful.

In this shared expedition, we'll delve into goal-setting, breaking it down into manageable steps, and unleashing the power within you to turn dreams into reality. So, ready your compass, dreams, and a sprinkle of stardust because, my friends, confidence in your future awaits on the voyage of your goals!

SMARTER Goal Technique

Define a specific, measurable, achievable, relevant, and time-bound goal, for your academics. Break it down into actionable steps with assigned deadlines, anticipate obstacles and develop strategies to overcome them, track progress, seek accountability, and regularly review and adjust your goals. And don't forget to reward yourself for how much you've accomplished!

Example: I will increase my Physics grade from an 82 to a 90 by attending tutoring twice per week. I will evaluate my progress weekly and as a reward will treat myself to an ice cream cone from my favorite parlor!

PACT Goal Technique

PACT stands for "Purposeful, Actionable, Continuous, and Trackable." This goal-setting approach introduces a unique perspective that emphasizes the significance of adding meaning and depth to your goals. Let's look at a couple of examples then you try.

Purposeful

Ensure that your goals have a clear and meaningful purpose. Understand why the goal is important to you and how it aligns with your values and aspirations.

Example: If the goal is to improve public speaking skills, the purpose could be to boost self-confidence, enhance communication abilities, or prepare for future academic or professional opportunities.

Actionable

Make your goals actionable by breaking them down into specific, doable tasks or steps. This ensures that you have a clear plan of action to follow.

Example: Instead of a vague goal like "improve fitness," make it actionable by setting specific tasks such as "exercise for 30 minutes three times a week" or "attend a fitness class every Monday."

Continuous
Encourage an ongoing commitment to your goals. Emphasize the importance of consistency and maintaining effort over time rather than viewing goals as one-time achievements.

Example: If the goal is to learn a new language, commit to daily practice or regular language exchange sessions to ensure continuous progress.

Trackable
Goals should be measurable and trackable to monitor progress. Define specific criteria or metrics that allow you to assess how well you are advancing toward your goal.

Example: If the goal is to save money, make it trackable by setting a specific savings target each month and regularly reviewing your babysitting deposits.

All right, imagine you want to learn a different language... Italian is fun... let's craft **SMARTER** and **PACT** goals for becoming Italian maestros:

SMARTER Goal:
Imagine this: You chatting away in Italian like a pro. That's our dream! Now, let's make it SMARTER:

Specific: Nail basic Italian conversations in six months.
Measurable: Hit those language modules, join language exchange sessions, and track your Italian superhero skills.
Achievable: 30 minutes daily, apps, and chats with native speakers – you got this!
Relevant: Dive into Italian for the love of culture and future travel dreams.
Time-Bound: Conquer Italian within six months, and check your progress regularly.
Evaluate: Quiz time! Assess your skills with language exchange sessions, quizzes, and a bit of self-reflection.
Reward: Look how far you've come. Hooray! Celebrate with a trip to your favorite Italian restaurant and *buon appetito!*

VS.

PACT Goal:

Let's infuse purpose into your Italian quest:
- **Purposeful:** Connect with Italian heritage and culture, growing personally through language.
- **Actionable:** Dive into daily practice – vocab, grammar, and lively chats with native speakers.
- **Continuous:** Italian isn't just a language; it's a lifestyle. Label stuff, chat while cooking – make it part of your daily groove.
- **Trackable:** Keep tabs on your Italian prowess with assessments – listening, speaking, and writing.

By adopting a **SMARTER goal**, you outline specific, measurable, achievable, relevant, and time-bound elements to ensure a structured and effective language learning plan. You also evaluate and reward yourself. The **PACT goal** emphasizes the purpose behind the goal, actionable steps, the importance of continuous effort, and the ability to track progress.

Both approaches offer a comprehensive strategy for achieving the goal of learning Italian.

WOOP Goal Technique

WOOP Goals. All right, teens, welcome to the world of WOOP – not the sound an owl makes, but a goal-setting magic trick brought to you by psychologist Gabriele Oettingen. WOOP stands for **Wish, Outcome, Obstacle, and Plan** – the roadmap to turn your wishes into tangible victories. Here's the lowdown:

Wish:
First things first, pick a wish or goal that makes your heart race a bit. It should be a challenge, but not climbing-Mount-Everest level. Think, "I wish to nail regular workouts and rock a healthy lifestyle."

Outcome:
- Now, close your eyes and imagine the sweet taste of success. Envision how achieving your goal will bring a wave of awesome benefits – like better fitness, a boost of energy, and an overall sense of "I'm crushing it!"

- **Obstacle:** Time to face the music. Identify the obstacles or sneaky challenges that might try to trip you up. Be real with yourself. Maybe it's a jam-packed schedule or the lure of the comfiest couch ever.

- **Plan:** But wait, we're not stopping there! Craft a plan, a battle strategy against those obstacles. If a hectic schedule is your nemesis, schedule workouts like VIP appointments, set reminders, and recruit a workout buddy for the ultimate accountability squad.

The **WOOP technique** is like having a stardust in a bottle. It's not just about wishful thinking; it's about balancing dreams with real-life planning. Use it by dreaming big, picturing success, acknowledging challenges, and crafting a battle plan, you're not just wishing upon a star – you're turning those wishes into your reality. Ready to **WOOP** your way to success and increase your confidence? Let's go!

HARD Goal Technique

The HARD goal-setting technique was introduced by Mark Murphy in his book "HARD Goals: *The Secret to Getting from Where You Are to Where You Want to Be.*" HARD goals... no, we're not talking about ones that make your life harder. HARD here stands for **Heartfelt, Animated, Required, and Difficult** – another way to turn your dreams into reality. Let's break it down:

Heartfelt:
This isn't about wishy-washy goals; it's about the ones that tug at your heartstrings. Think of goals that sync up with your values, passions, and sense of purpose. Forget "exercise more" – how about "boosting my energy levels so I can conquer the world"?

Animated:
Picture this: Your goals should be like a vivid, action-packed movie in your mind. Make them so clear that you can practically taste success. If your goal is running a marathon, imagine the thrill and pride as you cross that finish line.

- **Required:** No, it's not optional. Required goals are the MVPs that align with your bigger life plan. They're the stepping stones to personal or professional greatness. Need to save for college? Maybe a budget is in order.

- **Difficult:** But not impossible! Difficult goals are the spicy challenges that push you beyond your cozy comfort zone. No more easy-peasy goals like reading a book a month – how about acing a complex research project with a deadline breathing down your neck?

The **HARD goal-setting technique** isn't just some fancy jargon; it's your roadmap to success. It's about connecting emotionally with your goals, visualizing them in Technicolor, making sure they're non-negotiable for your big plan, and, of course, injecting a healthy dose of challenge. With HARD goals, you're not just setting goals; you're setting the stage for an epic journey of growth and accomplishment. Ready to rock those HARD goals, teens? Let's do this!

By wielding the mighty tools of **SMARTER, PACT, WOOP, and HARD goal techniques**, you're not just setting goals; you're crafting blueprints for your extraordinary future. These aren't just strategies; they're your companions, your trusty crew guiding you through uncharted waters.

Through the art of goal-setting, you're not shackled by uncertainty; you're the captain steering your ship through the seas of potential. Small victories become your treasure trove, and confidence, your precious loot.

So, why bother with this compass-guided odyssey? Because, dear revolutionaries, goal-setting isn't just about reaching destinations; it's about the thrilling journey, the lessons learned, and the growth experienced along the way. As you navigate your course, remember that the power to shape your destiny lies in your hands. Goal-setting isn't a mere tool; it's the secret that transforms dreams into reality, doubts into determination. So, go forth and set those goals; your adventure has just begun, and the horizon is yours to conquer!

SMARTER Goal Technique

Instructions: Define a specific, measurable, achievable, relevant, and time-bound goal with a reward of your choice.

S

Specific
What exactly do you want to achieve?

M

Measurable
How will you track your advancement?

A

Attainable
Evaluate the feasibility of your goal.

R

Relevant
How does it fit into your broader objectives?

T

Time-bound
What is the deadline?

E

Evaluate
How will you check on yourself?

R

Reward
Celebrate your milestones! How will you celebrate?

PACT Goal Technique

Instructions: Define a purposeful, actionable, continuous, and trackable goal of your choice.

P — Purposeful: Why is this important to you?

A — Actionable: What is your plan of action?

C — Continuous: How will you be consistent over time?

T — Trackable: How will you measure your progress?

WOOP Goal Technique

Instructions: Define a wish, outcome, obstacle, and plan goal of your choice.

W — Wish: Articulate a meaningful, challenging, but achievable wish.

O — Outcome: What feelings and benefits will it bring to your life?

O — Obstacle: What things might get in your way?

P — Plan: What actions will you take to address challenges?

HARD Goal Technique

Instructions: Define a heartfelt, animated, required, difficult goal of your choice.

H — Heartfelt

Articulate a meaningful goal aligned to your values.

A — Animated

Create a clear mental image of success; how do you feel? What do you visualize?

R — Required

What things are crucial to accomplish?

D — Difficult

What will push you out of your comfort zone to persevere?

Resilience Muscles

Picture this: Life is your mountain, and with every hurdle, up or down, you're not just climbing; you're gaining resilience, adaptability, and a belief that you can tackle any summit. It's like ascending the Everest of self-discovery!

As a teen, challenges aren't roadblocks; they're stepping stones. Each test, each trial is a chance to evolve, adapt, and emerge not just unscathed but stronger than ever. It's the transformative process, the crucible where your character gets forged. Picture it as your *superhero origin story* – adversity is the cosmic storm that grants you super resilience powers.

Now, why is resilience crucial? Well, it's your mental and emotional armor. When life throws curveballs, and adulting becomes a rollercoaster, that resilience becomes your shield. Remember those times when challenges seemed insurmountable? You conquered them! That's resilience flexing its muscles. And guess what? It's a secret weapon for building confidence.

Take some time and journal about times when you have overcome challenges. How did you conquer them? How did you become different as a result?

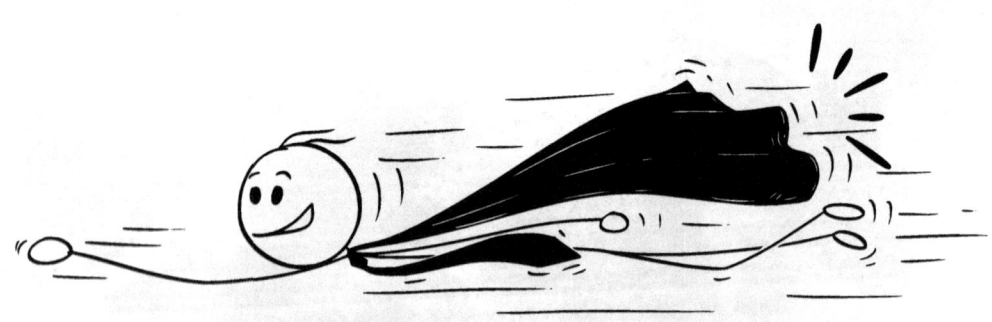

Strength Stones

In this activity, you'll craft and personalize "Strength Stones" – tangible reminders of your resilience that you can carry with you through life's ebbs and flows.

Materials Needed:

Smooth, flat stones (small to medium-sized)
Acrylic paint or paint pens
Paintbrushes
Water cup and palette
Fine-tip permanent markers
Clear sealant spray (optional)

Activity Steps:

Select Your Stones:
Begin by selecting stones that resonate with you. Each stone represents a challenge you've faced or an aspect of your inner strength you want to enhance.

Clean and Prepare:
Wash the stones thoroughly and let them dry. This cleansing process symbolizes leaving behind any negativity or past challenges, creating a fresh canvas for your artwork.

Visualize Your Strengths:
Close your eyes and reflect on the strengths and qualities that have helped you overcome challenges. Are you resilient, determined, or compassionate? Envision these traits as colors, shapes, or symbols.

Paint Your Stones:
Use acrylic paint or paint pens to bring your vision to life on each stone. You can paint words, symbols, or abstract designs that represent your inner strengths. Feel free to experiment with colors and patterns.

Add Personal Touches:
Use fine-tip permanent markers to add detailed touches or personal affirmations to your stones. Make them uniquely yours, expressing the essence of your resilience.

Let Them Dry:
Allow your stones to dry completely before moving on to the next step. This is a great time to reflect on the symbolic transformation taking place.

Optional Sealant:
If you'd like to preserve your artwork, consider applying a clear sealant spray. This protects the paint and ensures your Strength Stones withstand the test of time.

Arrange Your Stones:
Once dry, arrange your Strength Stones in a meaningful way. You might create a circle, a spiral, or any pattern that feels significant to you.

Hold and Reflect:
Hold your Strength Stones in your hands. Feel the texture, weight, and positive energy emanating from them. Take a moment to reflect on the journey you've traveled and the resilience you've cultivated.

Carry Your Strength:
Keep your Strength Stones in your pocket, bag, or a special place. Whenever you face a challenge, hold them close, reminding yourself of your inner strength and resilience.

May your Strength Stones be constant companions on your journey, reminding you of the indomitable strength within!

Growth Mindset

Envision your mindset as a majestic forest, with roots interwoven in a dance of determination beneath the forest floor. Growth mindset is the intricate network of roots, that draws strength from the belief that challenges are the essential nutrients for the towering trees of your personal and intellectual growth.

Picture two saplings in this metaphorical forest – one adorned with the vibrant leaves of a growth mindset, the other weighed down by the rigid branches of a fixed mindset. The growth mindset tree, reaching for the sun of possibilities, sees challenges as nutrients for its expanding canopy.

On the flip side, the fixed mindset tree, confined by its rigid branches, may shrink from challenges, viewing them as ominous storms threatening its very existence. Its growth is stunted, leaves rustling with doubts about the potential to evolve.

Cultivating a growth mindset is akin to tending to your mental garden, where the branches of your mindset tree stretch toward the heavens. These branches, illuminated with the wisdom of growth, bend and sway with the winds of challenges, knowing that each gust propels them toward new heights. As the gardener of your mind, you hold the shears that cut away limiting beliefs, allowing your mindset branches to reach even further.

In the rich soil of your experiences, imagine the resilience within you as sturdy roots, burrowing deep into the earth. These roots, anchor you firmly when the winds of challenge attempt to sway your branches. Resilience, nurtured by the strength of these roots, turns setbacks into fertile soil for growth.

Cultivating a growth mindset is a powerful tool that can build your resilience and shape the course of your adolescent years and beyond.

Tree of Growth

Use the illustration of the tree where the trunk represents your current abilities, and the branches represent areas of growth write a few in.

Roots of Reflection:
Label the roots with aspects of yourself that you believe are innate or fixed, such as talents or skills you feel you were born with. Take a moment to reflect on these aspects.

Branches of Growth:
On the branches, write down areas where you'd like to grow or improve. These could include skills, habits, or personal qualities you want to develop. These represent the growth opportunities.

Leaves of Effort:
As leaves are essential for a tree's growth, write down specific efforts you can make to nurture each area of growth. These efforts could include setting goals, seeking guidance, or practicing at something regularly.

Stormy Weather:
Introduce some "stormy weather" by discussing challenges or setbacks you might face while trying to grow in these areas. Write these challenges on the clouds around the tree.

Strategies for Weathering Storms:
Now brainstorm strategies to weather these storms. What can you do when faced with challenges? Write these strategies near the corresponding challenges.

Periodically revisit the *Tree of Growth*. Reflect on the progress made, celebrate successes, and adjust goals or strategies if needed. This ongoing reflection reinforces the idea that growth is continuous and helps you visualize your journey of growth and resilience.

Strategies For Success

The Power Of Yet

The Power of Yet is a mindset and concept developed within the framework of a growth mindset. It involves adding the word "yet" to the end of a statement to transform a fixed mindset into a growth mindset. The idea is to acknowledge that certain skills, abilities, or accomplishments may not have been achieved "yet," emphasizing the potential for future development and learning.

Here's how it works:

Fixed Mindset Statement: *"I can't do this."*
Growth Mindset Statement with the Power of Yet: *"I can't do this yet."*

By adding "yet," you shift your perspective from a belief that your current abilities are fixed to recognizing that you are on a journey of growth and development. This small addition will encourage a positive outlook and foster resilience in the face of challenges.

This mindset has three secret ingredients, each unlocking a different aspect of your untapped potential.

Optimism:
Picture challenges as temporary visitors on your journey, not permanent residents. With the *Power of Yet*, you'll see setbacks as mere pit stops, each offering a chance to stretch your mental muscles.

Persistence:
Meet your loyal sidekick, Persistence. Persistence is your guide through the twists and turns of learning, reminding you that the journey might be challenging, but the destination is worth the effort.

Belief in Potential:
Imagine your potential as a treasure chest waiting to be discovered. The Power of Yet flings open the lid, revealing the jewels within. With each "yet," you're adding gems to your collection—knowledge, skills, and wisdom. It's the belief that your potential isn't fixed. Together, let's turn every "I can't" into a resounding *"I can't yet, but I'm on my way!"*

I Believe In The Power Of Yet

Think of things that you want to learn. Write down all of your *I can't yet!* statements below. Everything you feel you can't do, know, and be. Don't forget the magic word!

Pick a few of these statements and think of ways you can plan to achieve them.

_____
_____
_____
_____
_____

Yet-o-Meter

Identify Three Challenges:
List three challenges or goals you've encountered recently.

Challenge 1: _____

Challenge 2: _____

Challenge 3: _____

Yet-o-Meter Scale:
Use the Yet-o-Meter scale for each challenge. Use the numbers 1 to 10, where 1 represents "Not started" and 10 represents "Mastered." Each time you level up, color in a square. Be sure to check with yourself and your challenges often.

1	1	1
2	2	2
3	3	3
4	4	4
5	5	5
6	6	6
7	7	7
8	8	8
9	9	9
10	10	10

Space To Journal

Space To Journal

The Power of Connection

Embarking on the tumultuous journey of adolescence can often feel like overcoming struggles like your favorite anime protagonist, filled with unexpected challenges. Yet, during challenges, social connections emerge as beacons of light, guiding you through the maze of life. More than just companionship, these connections become an invaluable support system, offering solace, resilience, and the strength to face even the toughest obstacles.

Consider the scenario of grappling with a seemingly insurmountable school project. The frustration mounts, and you're at a loss for solutions. Enter a friend—the sounding board whose fresh perspective transforms the unsolvable puzzle into a manageable challenge. Conversations with peers become catalysts for new ideas, providing a lifeline when navigating the complexities of academic endeavors.

In moments of despair, a simple, "*You will get through this*," becomes a powerful reminder that the journey is shared, and no one faces adversity alone. The strength drawn from these connections can be the deciding factor between succumbing to despair and finding the courage to persevere.

Life's journey is enriched by the shared experiences of a community. Learning from the trials and triumphs of those who have walked similar paths before offers a shortcut to wisdom.

Relationships that offer support, wisdom, hope, and a renewed sense of purpose become the cornerstone of building confidence. A community standing side by side serves as a reminder that the teenage journey... your journey, though challenging, does not need to be walked in isolation.

Together, as part of a supportive network, you can find the strength to navigate the maze of adolescence, emerging resilient and confident on the other side.

Mapping Your Support System

Instructions: Reflect on the people in your life who serve as trusted social connections. Answer the following questions to identify and appreciate the depth of your support network.

Family:
List family members who provide support.
Describe how each family member contributes to your well-being.

_____
_____
_____
_____

Friends:
Name close friends who stand by you.
Share specific instances when a friend has offered support.

_____
_____
_____
_____

Mentors/Role Models:
Identify mentors or role models in your life.
Explain how they inspire and guide you.

_____
_____
_____
_____

Teachers/Classmates:
Recognize teachers or classmates who contribute positively.
Note instances where their support has been impactful.

_____

_____

_____

_____

Online Connections:
Acknowledge supportive individuals in your online community.
Describe the nature of your connection and how it benefits you.

_____

_____

_____

_____

Consider **other sources of support** like pets, coaches, or neighbors.
Describe the unique support these individuals or elements offer.
Reflection:

_____

_____

_____

_____

What patterns or commonalities do you observe in the types of support you receive? How can you express gratitude and strengthen these connections?

Note: Feel free to customize this worksheet to include additional categories or questions based on your personal experiences and relationships.

_____
_____
_____
_____
_____
_____
_____
_____
_____
_____
_____
_____
_____
_____
_____
_____
_____
_____
_____
_____
_____
_____

Passions and Dreams

Passion is like this intense, burning enthusiasm or excitement you feel deep inside when you're doing something you love. It's that thing that makes your eyes light up and your heart beat faster. Unearthing your passion is like going on a treasure hunt for the activities or interests that make you lose track of time because you enjoy them so much.

Here's a cool way to find it: Allow yourself to first... dream. Imagine you have a magic wand, and with this wand, you can do anything you want. What would you choose to do? What activities make you forget about time or even forget to check your phone? Those moments might hold clues to your passions. It could be anything – drawing, playing an instrument, helping others, solving problems, or even creating something entirely new.

Dreams are like seeds; they hold the potential to sprout into passions. So, here's the deal: make time for your dreams. Set aside moments to let your thoughts wander and explore the "what ifs."

Imagine you're an inventor, an artist, an explorer, or whatever feels exciting. What are you doing in these dream scenarios? What activities bring you joy, satisfaction, or a sense of purpose? These dreamy adventures can be the stepping stones to uncovering your passions. Remember, every big thing starts with a little dream, and yours might just be the key to unlocking your unique passions.

So, grab that imaginary wand and explore different activities. Pay attention to what makes you feel alive and excited. Your passion is like your superpower, and once you discover it, it can add a whole lot of magic to your life!

Your space and time to dream....

The Role of Fear and Insecurity

As you take on the journey of building confidence, fear and insecurity often play significant roles, much like unexpected guests on an adventure. These emotions, while challenging, are not actually villains but rather side characters that can either hinder or propel the protagonist forward. Let's delve into their roles:

Fear: The Guardian of Comfort Zones
Fear tends to be the gatekeeper of comfort zones. It whispers doubts, raises uncertainties, and creates a protective bubble around what is familiar. As you step into the unknown territory of building confidence, fear might show up to ensure you think twice before leaping. It's not necessarily a foe but a cautious companion. Acknowledging fear's presence and understanding that it often signals growth can help you navigate past it. Sometimes, the very thing you fear holds the key to unlocking new levels of confidence.

Insecurity: The Mirror of Self-Perception
Insecurity acts like a mirror, reflecting your uncertainties and self-doubt. As you strive to build confidence, it might magnify perceived flaws or shortcomings, making you question your worth. However, insecurity is not a fixed state but a dynamic aspect of self-perception. It evolves as you do. Embracing your vulnerabilities and understanding that everyone, even the seemingly confident ones, grapples with insecurities at times can be a comforting realization. Instead of battling insecurities, see them as reminders of your humanity and opportunities for growth.

Overcoming Fear and Insecurity: The Hero's Journey
In the hero's journey of building confidence, the hero (that's you!) faces fears and insecurities head-on. Rather than suppressing these emotions, you acknowledge them, recognizing that they are part of the adventure. It's about transforming fear into courage and insecurity into self-acceptance. By embracing the discomfort, you grow stronger, more resilient, and gradually build the confidence to face whatever challenges lie ahead.

In essence, fear and insecurity are not enemies to be defeated but elements to be understood and integrated into your journey toward confidence. They shape your narrative, adding depth and complexity to your character. As you navigate through them, you become the hero of your story, with fear and insecurity serving as stepping stones toward greater self-assurance.

Create Your Teen Confidence Revolution Community

Your Guide to Community Building

Our dear revolutionaries! After all you have learned, done, and practiced in this workbook you are ready to unleash, share, and create your own *Teen Confidence Revolution Community* – that's awesome sauce! Crafting this space isn't just about ticking off to-dos; it's a journey to transform lives. Get ready to dive into the deets with our step-by-step guide to launching your very own *Teen Confidence Revolution Community* for fellow teens.

Step 1: Dream Big, Set the Tone

Picture this: you're at the helm of something epic. But first, define why you're doing this and what epic looks like. Are you creating a hub for shared experiences, mutual support, or a growth playground? Nail down the values that'll be the north star of your community.

Step 2: Rally Your Crew

Think of your dream team – friends, classmates, or peers who are all about leveling up in the confidence game. Surround yourself with like-minded peeps who can contribute to and benefit from the community.

Step 3: Choose Your Playground

Decide where the magic will happen – a buzzing social media group, a slick website, or good old face-to-face gatherings. Pick a platform that screams "us" and suits the vibe you're going for.

Step 4: Code of Conduct – Keep It Cool

Set some ground rules. Think of them as the signature element that ensures your community stays positive and drama-free. Make it crystal clear: respect, support, and mum's the word on confidentiality.

Step 5: Stir the Pot with Engaging Stuff
Plan content that fuels the fire. Think discussions, challenges, goal-setting escapades, and moments for sharing triumphs and hiccups. Spice things up regularly to keep your squad hooked.

Step 6: Roll Out the Red Carpet – Promo Time!
Let the world (or at least your world) know about your *Teen Confidence Revolution Community*. Social media, school announcements, or even good old-fashioned chatter – shout it from the rooftops. Highlight the perks of joining and the epic impact your crew's gonna make.

Step 7: Bring the Vibes – Foster Connections
Create a vibe where everyone feels comfy opening up, sharing, and lifting each other. Make your space a judgment-free zone where everyone's on a journey of their own.

Step 8: Game Day – Events and Activities
Plan events that are as cool as your community. Workshops, guest speakers, or joint projects – get the gang involved. These events are like the glue that keeps your community tight-knit and buzzing.

Step 9: Tune In – Seek Feedback and Rock On
Don't be shy – ask for feedback. What's working, what needs tweaking? Use this intel to keep your community fresh, rad, and always on point.

Step 10: It's a Party – Celebrate Wins
Cheers to victories, big or small! Shout-outs, fist bumps, virtual confetti – celebrate achievements that make your community shine. It's not just about the destination; it's about enjoying the ride.

So there you have it! Your *Teen Confidence Revolution Community* is more than a space; it's a movement. Most of the work in this book you have to complete on your own but it's much more fun to do with friends. Keep inspiring confidence and resilience in yourself and your tribe. Let's rock this revolution of positive change in teens everywhere!

We have come to the end of our journey together. We hope you have enjoyed the activities in this workbook and close this book renewed and inspired. As you stand on the summit of this transformative journey, take a moment to reflect on the incredible distance you've covered. You've navigated challenges, embraced your uniqueness, and cultivated resilience. Your commitment and effort in completing these exercises are not just commendable; they are worth celebrating.

Remember, this is not the end but a pivotal milestone in your ongoing adventure. The seeds of confidence you've planted will continue to bloom as you apply and practice what you've learned. Your evolution is an ongoing process, and with each step, you reshape the landscape of your life experience.

As you move forward, carry the magic within you. The world needs your unique contributions, your positivity, and your kindness. You've not just evolved; you've revolutionized your thinking and ways of being. You are now equipped to create a ripple effect of confidence, positivity, and transformative energy.

As you step into the next chapter of your life, remember that you are the embodiment of the *Teen Confidence Revolution*. Keep shining, keep evolving, and keep being the magical force that the world desperately needs. Your journey has just begun.

You have completed the workbook, fearless revolutionary! Find the **Teen Confidence Revolution Manifesto** on the next page, your daily reminder that you possess the power to transform uncertainty into strength, doubts into resilience, and dreams into reality.

Repeat these affirmations daily, and let the *Teen Confidence Revolution* unfold within you. You are not just a participant; you are a revolutionary, rewriting the script of your life with confidence, courage, and unwavering belief in your extraordinary potential. Stand tall, embrace your uniqueness, and let the world witness the force of your confidence.

I AM THE ARCHITECT OF MY DESTINY.

Today, I acknowledge that my path is shaped by my choices. I am not a mere spectator; I am the creator of my journey. Every decision I make contributes to the masterpiece of my life.

FEAR IS MY COMPANION, NOT MY CAPTOR.

Fear is a passenger on my journey, not the driver. I welcome its presence as a sign of growth. With every step I take in the face of fear, I expand my courage and fortify my confidence.

MY IMPERFECTIONS MAKE ME EXCEPTIONAL.

I celebrate my quirks, flaws, and imperfections. They are not blemishes but brushstrokes that paint the canvas of my uniqueness. I am a masterpiece in progress, constantly evolving and becoming.

TODAY, I WILL EMBRACE CHALLENGES AS OPPORTUNITIES.

Challenges are not roadblocks; they are invitations to grow. I face each challenge with a warrior's spirit, knowing that overcoming obstacles strengthens my resilience and fuels my confidence.

I AM THE AUTHOR OF MY STORY.

My story is not dictated by external voices but written by the pen in my hand. I choose narratives that uplift, inspire, and empower. In every chapter, I am the hero who rises, learns, and perseveres.

MY VOICE MATTERS; I WILL SPEAK WITH AUTHORITY.

I speak my truth with courage and conviction. My voice is a force for change, and I use it to uplift others and advocate for what I believe in. My words have power, and I wield them wisely.

I AM A CONSTANT LEARNER.

Knowledge is my ally in this revolution. I approach each day with a student's heart, eager to learn, adapt, and grow. I am a seeker of wisdom, and with every lesson, I become more confident.

TODAY, I WILL LIFT OTHERS AS I RISE.

I am not alone on this journey. As I ascend, I extend a helping hand to those around me. Together, we create a community of confidence, where each victory is shared, and every setback is a collective opportunity to rise stronger.

I AM A FORCE OF POSITIVITY AND KINDNESS.

In a world that sometimes feels chaotic, I choose to be a beacon of positivity and kindness. Small acts of kindness can spark revolutions, and I am the catalyst for positive change.

TODAY, I WILL LIVE WITH INTENTION.

I am not a passenger in my life; I am the driver. Today, I live with purpose and intention. Every action I take aligns with my values, aspirations, and the confident spirit that resides within me.

By leaving a review, you're not just sharing your opinion; **you're contributing to a movement that empowers teens** to reach their full potential.

If you're on Audible Hit the three dots at the top right of your device click rate and review, then leave a few sentences about the book with a star rating.

If you are on Kindle or an eReader scroll to the bottom of the book then swipe up and it will prompt you to leave a review.

If for some reason these instructions have changed, simply go to Amazon or wherever you purchase the book and leave a review right on the books page. For Amazon, click here.

Thank you from the Teen Powerhouse Society!

Your generosity is valued beyond measure. We can't wait to continue this journey with you, unlocking more strategies to boost self-esteem, reduce stress, and help you achieve your goals.

Remember, your review isn't just about a book; it's about creating a ripple effect of confidence that can change lives. So, thank you for being a part of something incredible!

Warm regards,
Teen Powerhouse Society

PS - Share the positivity! If you know someone who could benefit from this book, send it their way, and let's spread the teen confidence revolution together.

References

Alisha. (2017, November 5). 100 Quotes on Art & Creativity. Masterpiece Society. https://masterpiecesociety.com/100-quotes-art-creativity/

Association for Psychological Science. (2017, July 17). Asking Questions Increases Likability. https://www.psychologicalscience.org/news/minds-business/asking-questions-increases-likability.html

At Risk Youth Programs. (2023, March 31). Build Confidence & Overcoming Low Self-Esteem in Teenagers. https://atriskyouthprograms.com/low-self-esteem-in-teenagers-2/

Beautifully Simply You. (2019, February 4). Celebrate Your Uniqueness. https://beautifullysimplyyou.com/2019/02/04/celebrate-your-uniqueness/

Blount, S. (2019, March 2). Three Ways To Grow From Failure. Forbes. https://www.forbes.com/sites/sallyblount/2019/05/02/three-ways-to-grow-from-failure/?sh=73cc72b5666d

Brundin, J. (2019, December 2). Teen Diary: Amelia Tells Us How Academic Stress Led Her To A Breakdown. Colorado Public Radio. https://www.cpr.org/2019/12/02/teen-diary-amelia-tells-us-how-academic-stress-led-her-to-a-breakdown/

Castrillon, C. (2020, November 24). How To Stop Comparing Yourself To Others. Forbes. https://www.forbes.com/sites/carolinecastrillon/2020/11/24/how-to-stop-comparing-yourself-to-others/?sh=7fc8b88c6473

Deane, J. (2021, December 16). How To Reflect On The Past Year And Set Goals For The Year Ahead. LinkedIn. https://www.linkedin.com/pulse/how-reflect-past-year-set-goals-ahead-jennifer-deane-pcc-she-her-/

Derr, A. (2020, October 16). Social Connection Quotes. Visible Network Labs. https://visiblenetworklabs.com/2020/10/16/thirty-three-best-social-connection-quotes/

References

Difference Psychology. (2022, August 19). WOOP! https://differencepsychology.com.au/newsletters/f/woop

Eatough, E. (2022, January 7). How to say no to others (and why you shouldn't feel guilty). BetterUp. https://www.betterup.com/blog/how-to-say-no

Eatough, E. (2023, October 5). "We are the champions" plus other qualities every good friend should have. BetterUp. https://www.forbes.com/sites/sallyblount/2019/05/02/three-ways-to-grow-from-failure/?sh=73cc72b5666d

Emerson, M. (2023, February 6). 8 Tips For Better Communication Skills. Forbes. https://www.forbes.com/sites/harvard-division-of-continuing-education/2023/02/06/8-tips-for-better-communication-skills/?sh=7ec7e93a6993

Erieau, C. (2019, February 20). The 50 best resilience quotes. Hello Driven. https://home.hellodriven.com/articles/the-50-best-resilience-quotes/

Families for Life. (n.d.). How to Strengthen Your Extended Family Ties. https://ffl.familiesforlife.sg/pages/Article/How-to-Strengthen-Your-Extended-Family-Ties

Graham, L. (2016, September 16). 4 Ways to Find Your Unique Voice. Thrive Global. https://community.thriveglobal.com/4-ways-to-find-your-unique-voice/

Hailey, L. (n.d.). How to Set Boundaries: 5 Ways to Draw the Line Politely. Science of People. https://www.scienceofpeople.com/how-to-set-boundaries/

Hansen, L. (2015, January 9). 9 heroic teens and their incredible acts of bravery [Updated]. The Week. https://theweek.com/articles/468498/9-heroic-teens-incredible-acts-bravery-updated

References

Health Direct. (2022, July). Motivation: How to get started and staying motivated. https://www.healthdirect.gov.au/motivation-how-to-get-started-and-staying-motivated

Heather. (2019, November 30). The Importance of Connection for Adolescents. Heather Hayes & Associates. https://www.heatherhayes.com/the-importance-of-connection-for-adolescents/

Heckman, W. (2017). 6 Common Triggers of Teen Stress. The American Institute of Stress. https://www.stress.org/6-common-triggers-of-teen-stress

Hill, J. (2023, August 18). 14 Reasons To Always Try New Things in Life. LifeHack. https://www.lifehack.org/902478/try-new-things

Hundley, S. (2020, October 22). How to Make Time for More Fun! Mindful Counseling. https://mindfulcounselingutah.com/blog/2020/10/22/how-to-make-time-for-more-fun.

Hurley, K. (2022, June 14). What Is Resilience? Definition, Types, Building Resiliency, Benefits, and Resources. EverydayHealth.com. https://www.everydayhealth.com/wellness/resilience/

Kaminsky, A. (2016, September 16). Teens, Social Media And The Illusion Of Perfection. Pys-Ed. https://www.psy-ed.com/wpblog/teens-and-social-media/

Kristenson, S. (2022a, May 19). 11 Benefits of Developing a Growth Mindset in Life. Develop Good Habits. https://www.developgoodhabits.com/benefits-growth-mindset/

Kristenson, S. (2022b, June 2). 7 Proven Alternatives to SMART Goals. Develop Good Habits. https://www.developgoodhabits.com/smart-goals-alternative/

Latham, G., & Locke, E. (2007). New Developments in and Directions for Goal-Setting Research. European Psychologist 12(4):290-300 https://www.researchgate.net/publication/247399303_New_Developments_in_and_Directions_for_Goal-Setting_Research

References

Lauren. (2022, May 30). 100 Powerful Self Confidence Quotes for Girls. Simply Well Balanced. https://simply-well-balanced.com/confidence-quotes-for-girls/

Legg, T. (2021, January 27). Gut Feelings Are Real, but Should You Really "Trust Your Gut"? Healthline. https://www.healthline.com/health/mental-health/trust-your-gut

Machina, Z. (2022). 5 Dangers of Having a Fixed Mindset. PHASE. https://phase.undock.com/5-dangers-of-having-a-fixed-mindset/

Madill, E. (n.d.). How to Transform Challenges into Opportunities for Growth. Vunela. https://www.vunela.com/how-to-transform-challenges-into-opportunities-for-growth/

Magana, S., Morrow, D., Bird, M., Toribio, Y., & Khan, H. (2017). Student Success Stories. Student Success at The University of Utah. https://studentsuccess.utah.edu/advocates/student-success-stories/

Martinez, N. (2023, March 7). 5 Reasons You Should Unplug From Social Media. CNET. https://www.cnet.com/health/mental/unplug-from-social-media/

May, L. (2023, September 7). Is confidence inherited or a learned skill? LinkedIn. https://www.linkedin.com/pulse/confidence-inherited-learned-skill-lisa-may-gaicd

Moore, C. (2019, March 4). Positive Daily Affirmations: Is There Science Behind It? Positive Psychology. https://positivepsychology.com/daily-affirmations/#research

MyMnCareers. (n.d.). Long-Term and Short-Term Goals. https://careerwise.minnstate.edu/mymncareers/finish-school/long-short-goals.html

Parenting Teens and Tweens. (2023, May 31). 24 Inspiring Quotes to Help Your Anxious Teenager. https://parentingteensandtweens.com/best-quotes-for-anxious-teens/

References

Patel, S. (2020, June 19). The 12 Morning Rituals That Help to Kick Off Successful Days. The Muse. https://www.themuse.com/advice/the-12-morning-rituals-that-help-to-kick-off-successful-days

Pederson, T. (2023, February 27). How Does Social Media Affect Body Image? PsychCentral. https://psychcentral.com/health/how-the-media-affects-body-image

Price-Mitchell, M. (2018, June 26). Self-Awareness Quotes That Help Kids Explore Their Inner Selves. Roots of Action. https://www.rootsofaction.com/self-awareness-quotes/

Putman, P., Antypa, N., Crysovergi, P., & van der Does, W. A. J. (2009). Exogenous cortisol acutely influences motivated decision making in healthy young men. Psychopharmacology, 208(2), 257–263. https://doi.org/10.1007/s00213-009-1725-y

Raising Healthy Teens. (2019, December 31). Tips to Help Your Teen Cultivate Their Passion. https://raisinghealthyteens.org/tips-to-help-your-teen-cultivate-their-passion/

ReachOut. (n.d.). Stress and teenagers. https://parents.au.reachout.com/common-concerns/everyday-issues/stress-and-teenagers

Restless Development. (2020, August 11). Four stories of youth resilience from around the world. https://restlessdevelopment.org/2020/08/four-stories-of-youth-resilience-from-around-the-world/

Richardson, T. (2020, September 18). 6 Actionable Ways To Find & Speak Your Truth. Mind Body Green. https://www.mindbodygreen.com/articles/how-to-find-and-speak-your-truth

Rood, E. (2020, October 13). Building Self-Awareness and Emotional Intelligence in Teens. Inspire Balance. https://www.inspirebalance.com/eq-self-awareness-teens/

References

Rusack, P. (2023, January 4). 69 Inspirational Goal-Setting Quotes. We Are Teachers. https://www.weareteachers.com/goal-setting-quotes/

Sabrina. (2023, October 27). 7 Quotes about Insecurity for Teens. All Womens Talk. https://teen.allwomenstalk.com/quotes-about-insecurity-for-teens/

Salameh, S. (2023, May 24). Young dreamers making a difference in their communities. UNICEF. https://www.unicef.org/syria/stories/young-dreamers-making-difference-their-communities

Self Esteem School. (n.d.). Some Interesting Self Esteem Statistics and Fact You Might Not Be Aware Of. https://www.self-esteem-school.com/self-esteem-statistics.html

Shonk, K. (2023, July 31). What is Conflict Resolution, and How Does It Work? Program on Negotiation; Harvard Law School. https://www.pon.harvard.edu/daily/conflict-resolution/what-is-conflict-resolution-and-how-does-it-work/

Slumber Kins. (2020, February 28). One in 7.7 Billion: Raising Children to be Their Authentic Self. https://slumberkins.com/blogs/slumberkins-blog/one-in-7-7-billion

Smamore Castle. (2023, July 4). 12 Ways to Overcome Your Mindless Scrolling Habit. https://www.smarmore-rehab-clinic.com/blog/addiction-advice/12-ways-to-overcome-your-mindless-scrolling-habit/

StopBullying. (2019, September 24). Facts about bullying. Department of Health and Human Services. https://www.stopbullying.gov/resources/facts

Thomas, T. (2023, July 20). Embracing My Unique Difference: A Journey as a Dextrocardian. Medium. https://medium.com/@theretaleacademy/embracing-my-unique-difference-a-journey-as-a-dextrocardian-b919279bf65dT

References

Victoria University. (n.d.). How to make an effective study plan. Victoria University Melbourne Australia. https://www.vu.edu.au/about-vu/news-events/study-space/how-to-make-an-effective-study-plan

Vogt, C. (2021, September 1). Under Pressure: Are the Stresses of Social Media Too Much for Teens and Young Adults? Everyday Health. https://www.everydayhealth.com/emotional-health/under-pressure/are-the-stresses-of-social-media-too-much-for-teens-and-young-adults/

Walsh, E. (2022, October 27). Teens and Screens: Why The Shift From Control to Connection is Key to Mental Health. Spark & Stitch Institute. https://sparkandstitchinstitute.com/teens-and-screens-why-the-shift-from-control-to-connection-is-key-to-mental-health/

Wilding, M. (2021, December 13). 5 Myths About Confidence That Are Making You More Insecure. Forbes. https://www.forbes.com/sites/melodywilding/2021/12/13/5-myths-about-confidence-that-are-making-you-more-insecure/?sh=4e2eeca7bbf1

Williams, J. (2018, September 4). Developing Adolescent Identity. Parent and Teen. https://parentandteen.com/developing-adolescent-identity/

Wisal, K. (2019, October 15). Insecurities Among Teenagers. Medium. https://medium.com/@kashifawisal786/insecurities-among-teenagers-2f40631e53ba

Illustrations: Canva Pro zdeneksasek

Printed in Great Britain
by Amazon